SCHULTZ Piano Course

by

Pamela and Robert Schultz

To Teachers and Parents —

The Schultz Piano Course is a comprehensive, flexible course of music instruction for the young, beginning piano student. It is easily adapted to each student's individual rate of progress. The complete course includes three areas of study - reading and performance, technique, and theory - to be studied simultaneously in the piano lesson. Each area is covered in three carefully graded levels to encourage logical and steady progress.

The Technique books provide a solid foundation in finger strength and finger independence, with emphasis on equal development of each hand. Finger drills are supplemented with studies in other important areas of piano technique. Additional activities requiring repetition and transposition encourage the student's musical awareness and creativity while providing a well-rounded piano technique.

Parents — encourage, share and enjoy your child's music training. The rewards can last a lifetime.

Design and Illustration - Thomas Wharton / Editors - Pamela and Robert Schultz / Production - Frank J. Hackinson

Introduction

It is very important to learn to play from the beginning with a GOOD HAND POSITION.

Hand Position

To find YOUR perfect hand position:

1. Sit straight (not rigid) at the piano with your shoulders, arms, wrists and hands relaxed at your sides. Your hands will be cupped slightly if they are relaxed.

2. Bend your right elbow, raise your hand and rest it on the keyboard with one key under each finger. Your forearm and wrist should be level.

3. Keep the relaxed hand position that you had at your side.

4. Repeat Steps 1-3 with your left hand.

This is your perfect hand position at the piano.

Always play with a quiet hand position, and with this NATURAL CURVE to the fingers.

Make a firm finger stroke with every finger.

Fallboard Exercises

The fallboard is the key cover on your piano.
Close the fallboard for these first warm-up exercises.
(A tabletop works too.)

Play each exercise SLOWLY, thinking about:

- Good hand position
- Firm finger stroke
- Steady pulse.

Follow the numbers for the fingers, with 1 for the thumbs.
Play each exercise with the right hand, then the left hand, then both hands.

1.

1 - 2 - 3 - 4 - 5 - 4 - 3 - 2 - repeat several times - end with 1.

2.

1 - 2 - 1 - 3 - 1 - 4 - 1 - 5 - 1 - 5 - 1 - 4 - 1 - 3 - 1 - 2 - repeat several times - end with 1.

3.

1 - 3 - 2 - 4 - 3 - 5 - 4 - 2 - repeat several times - end with 1.

Begin your daily practice for several weeks with these fallboard exercises.

As you practice the exercises on the following pages:

- keep a quiet, curved hand position,
- make a firm finger stroke to the bed (bottom) of every key so that the sound is medium loud,
- keep a steady pulse.

1. Getting Started — Right Hand

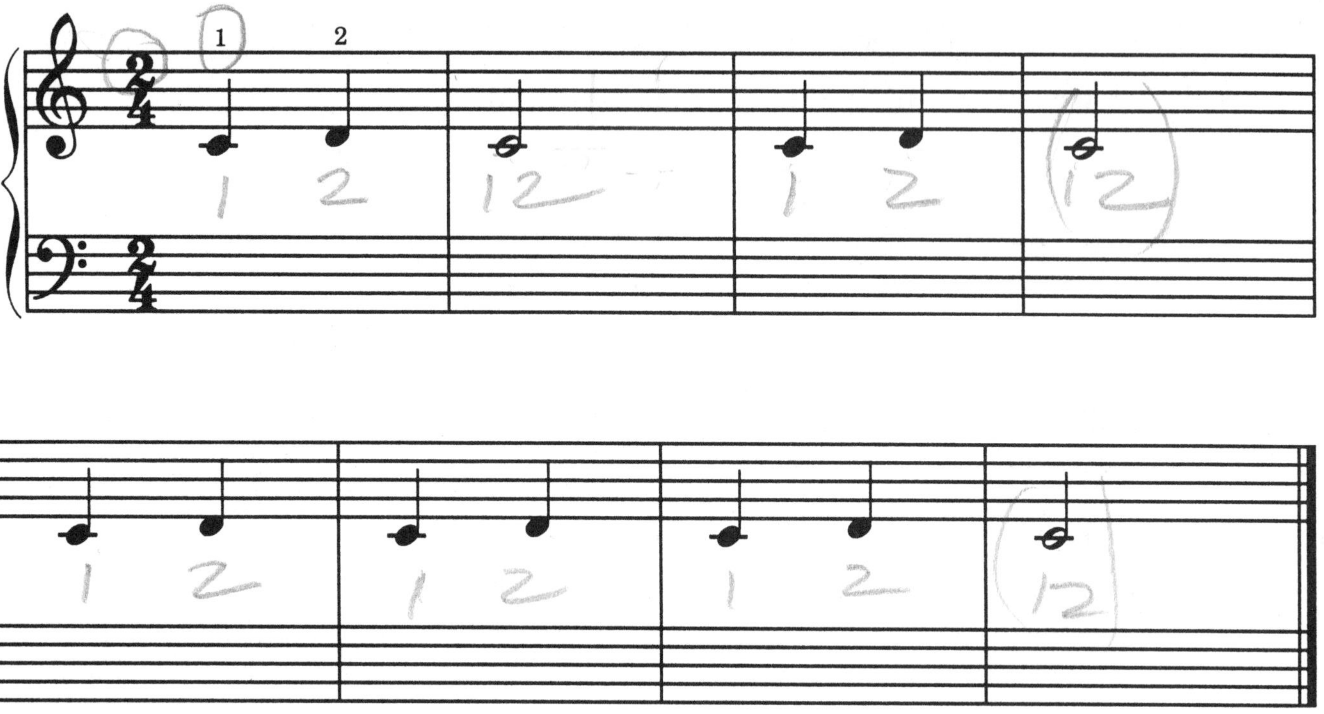

2. Getting Started — Left Hand

Variation: Play both exercises on this page as one exercise, without stopping at the first double bar.

3. Both Hands Now

4. Two Finger Workout

Variation for Number 4: Play the right hand higher, beginning on the next C above Middle C. Play the left hand as written.

5. Stepping Up and Down

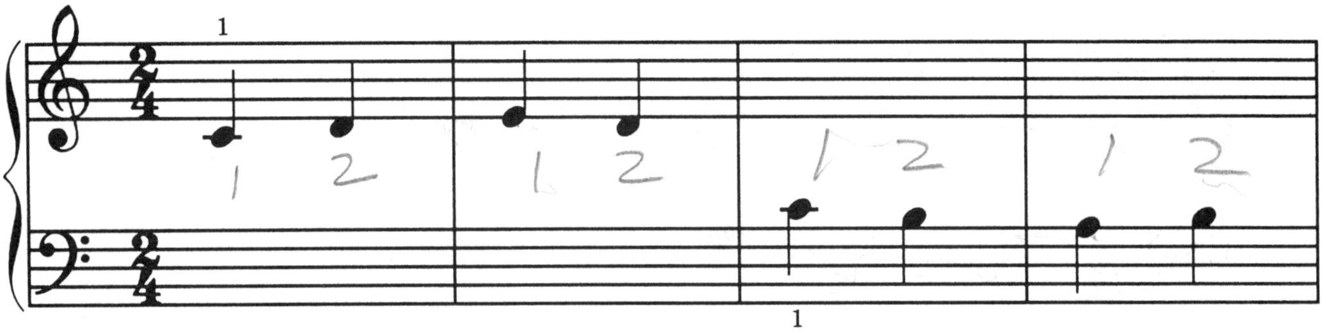

6. Three Finger Workout

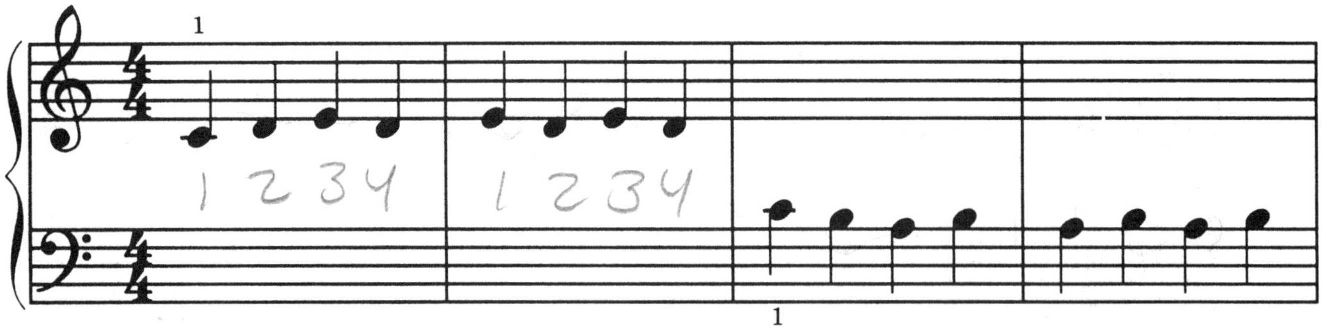

Variation for Number 6: Play the left hand lower, beginning on the next C below Middle C. Play the right hand as written.

7. Half Notes and Quarter Notes for Three Fingers

8. More Half Notes and Quarter Notes

9. Stepping Further Up and Down

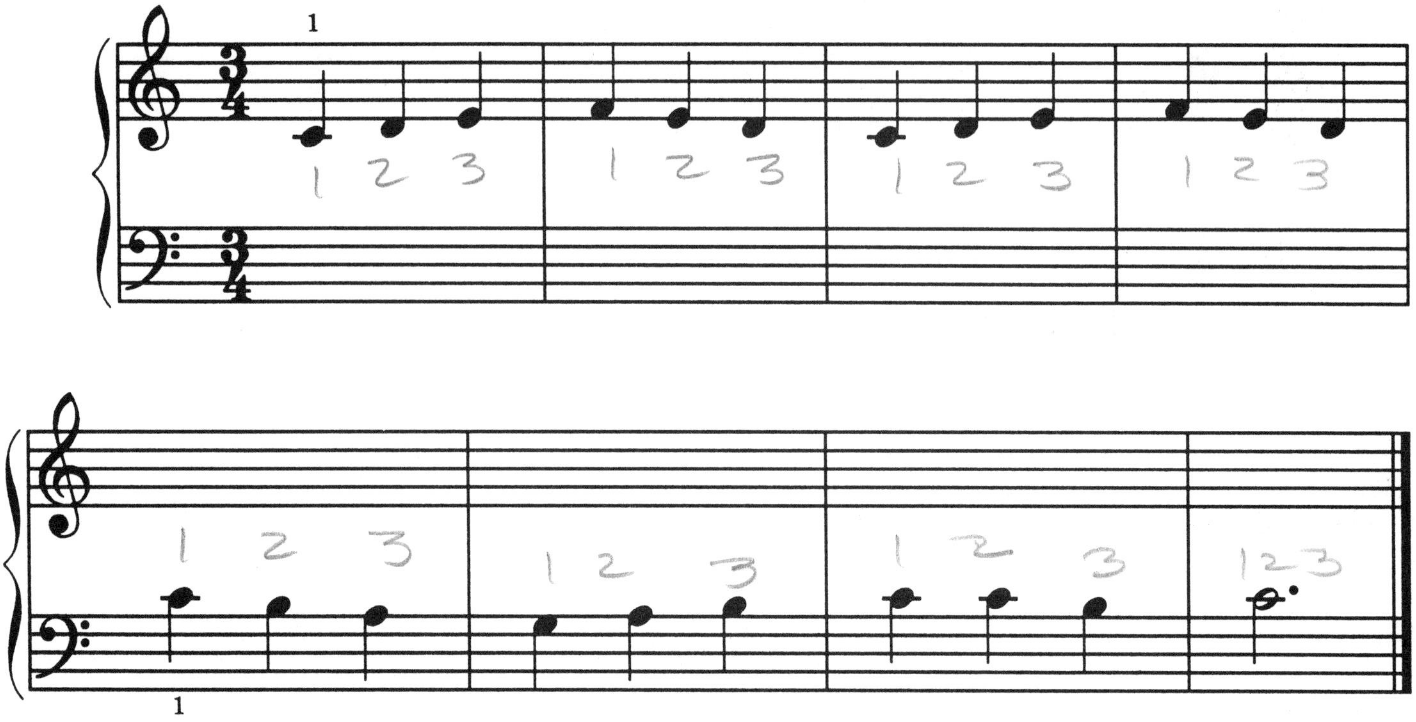

10. Four Finger Workout

Variation for Number 10: Play both hands higher, beginning on the next C above Middle C.

11. Four Finger Pattern in 4/4

12. Four Finger Pattern in 3/4

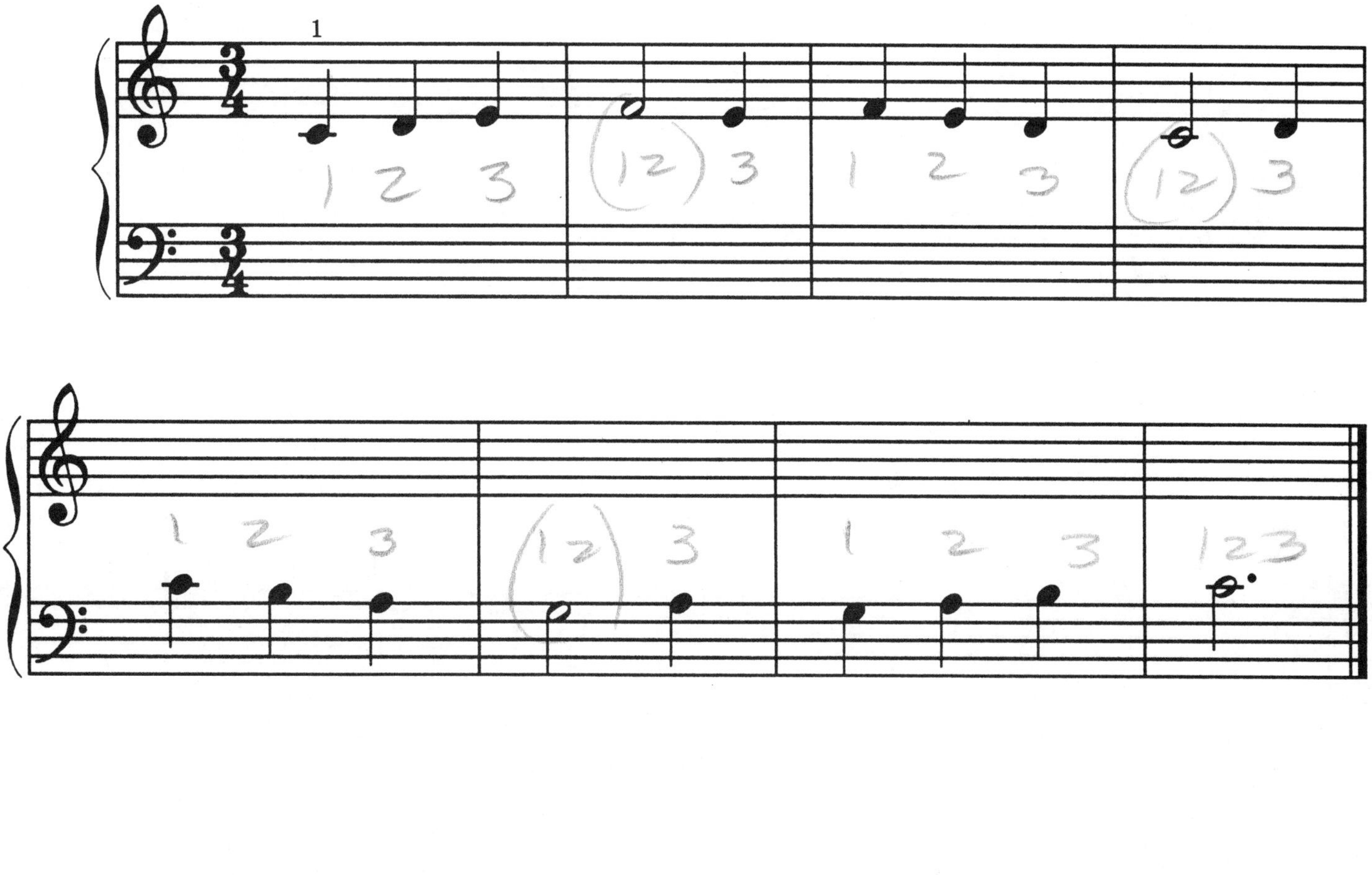

13. Stepping Out on All Five Fingers

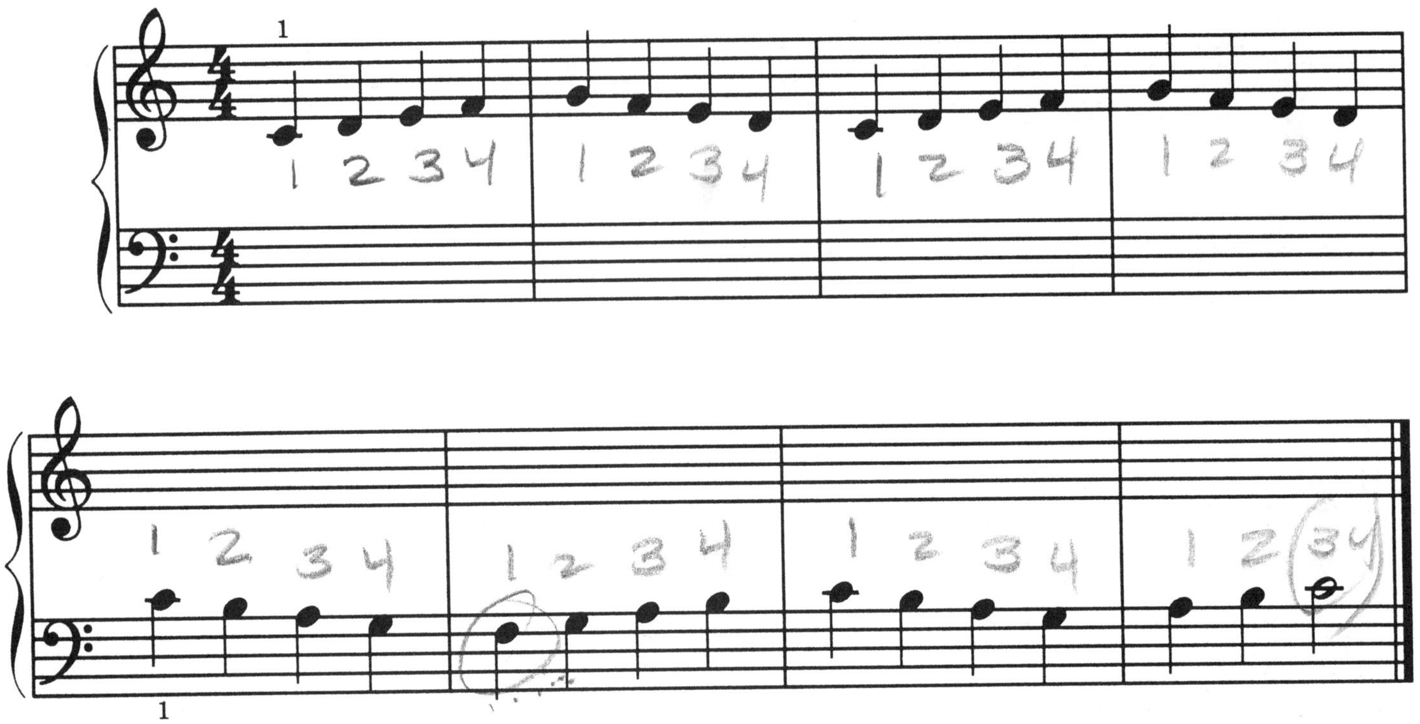

14. Left Hand Leader

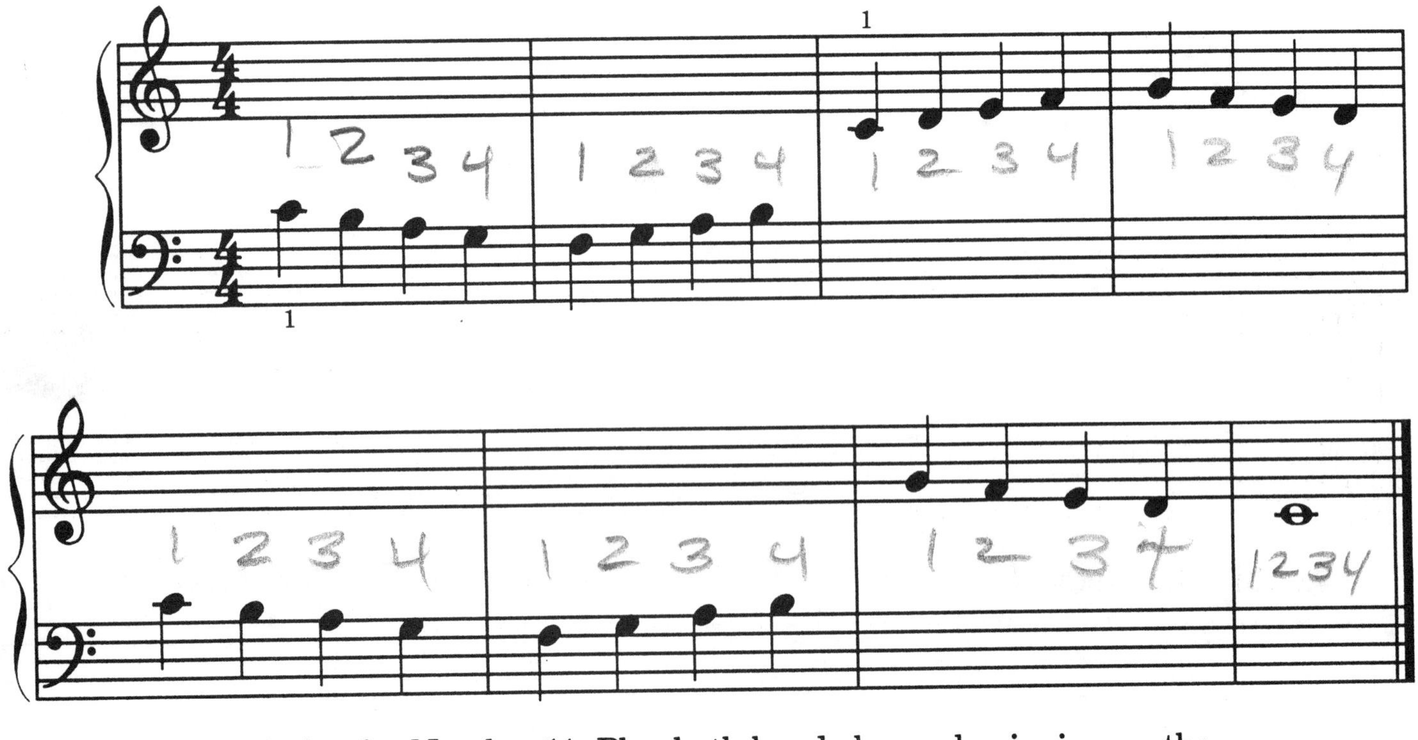

Variation for Number 14: Play both hands lower, beginning on the next C below Middle C.

15. Five Finger Workout

Variation for Number 15: Play the right hand higher and left hand lower, beginning on the next C's above and below Middle C.

16. Half Notes and Quarter Notes for Five Fingers

17. Five Finger Drill

Create your own variation for Number 17.

18. Five Finger Study

19. Skip Away from C

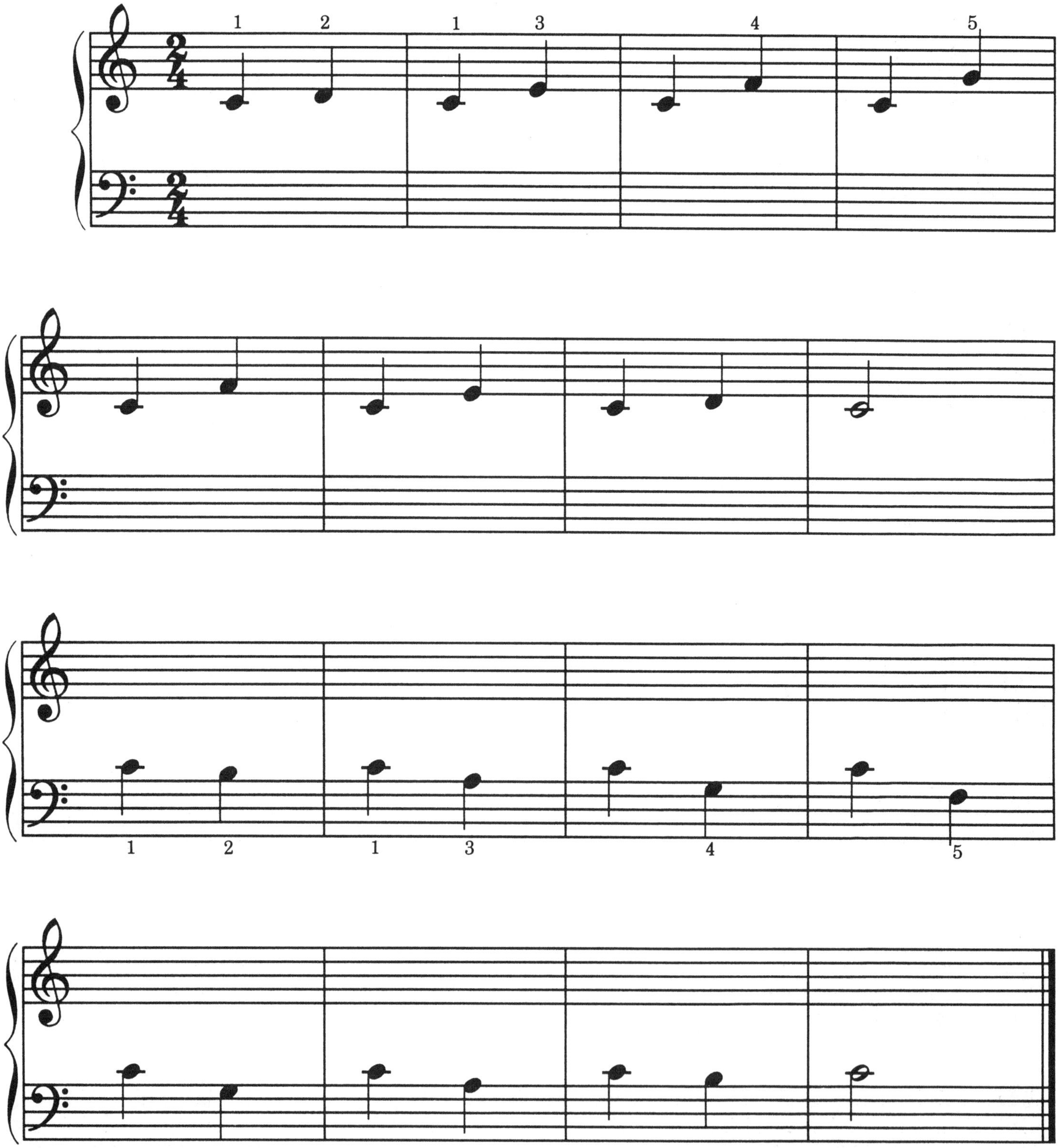

Variation for Number 19: Play the right hand two octaves higher, and the left hand two octaves lower than written.

20. Repeated Skips

21. Mixed Intervals

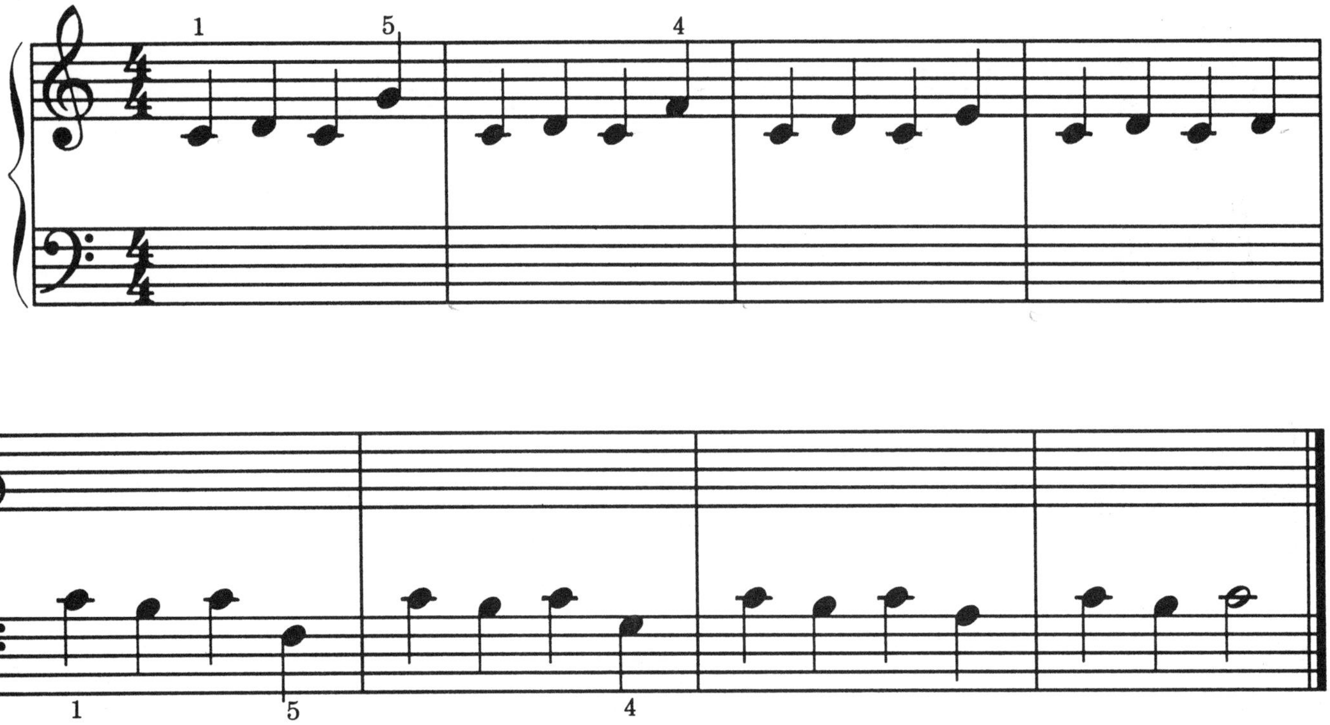

22. More Mixed Intervals

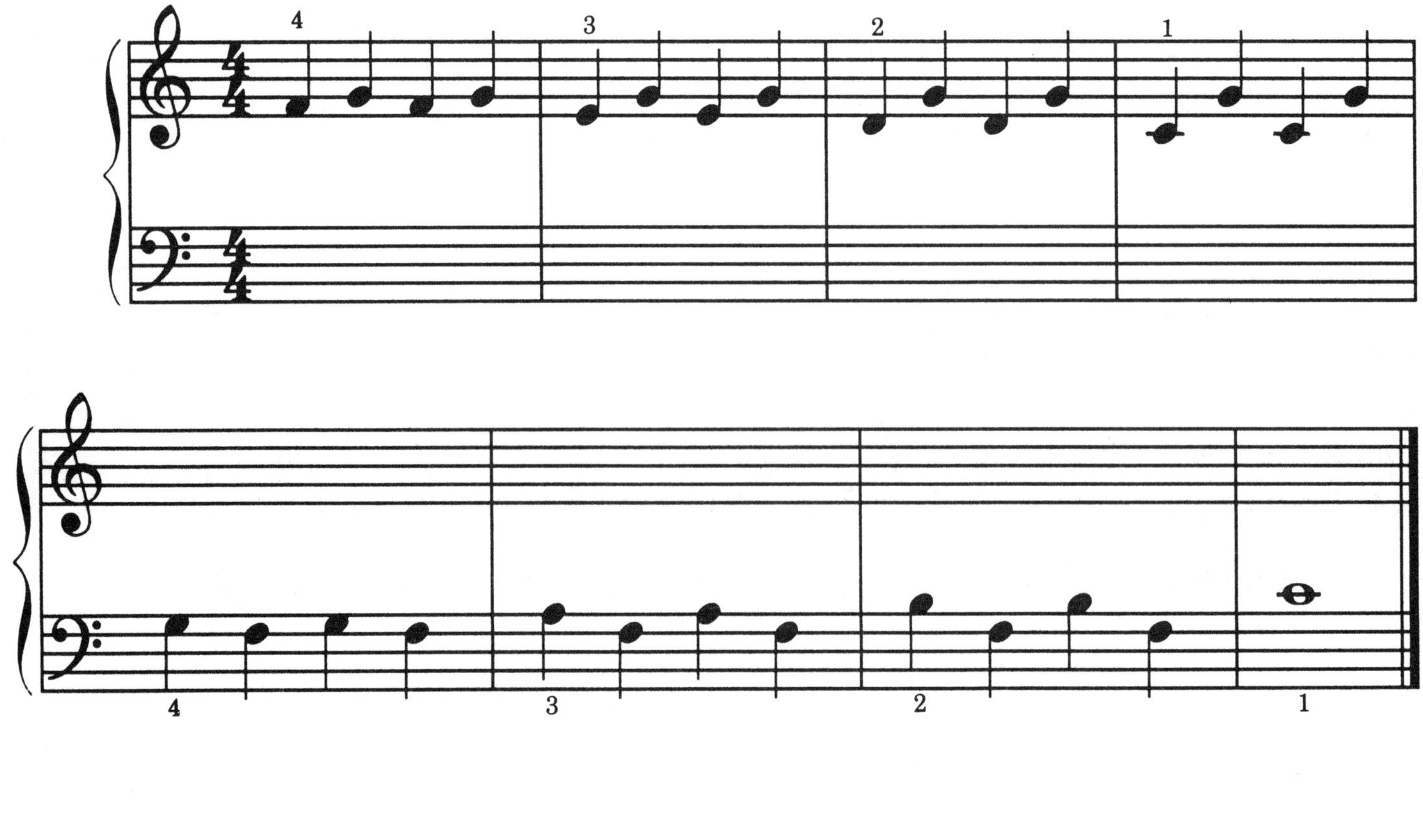

23. Mixed Interval Workout

Variation for Number 23: Play both hands two octaves higher than written.

24. Broken Thirds

25. Broken Thirds Follow the Leader

26. Broken Thirds in 3/4

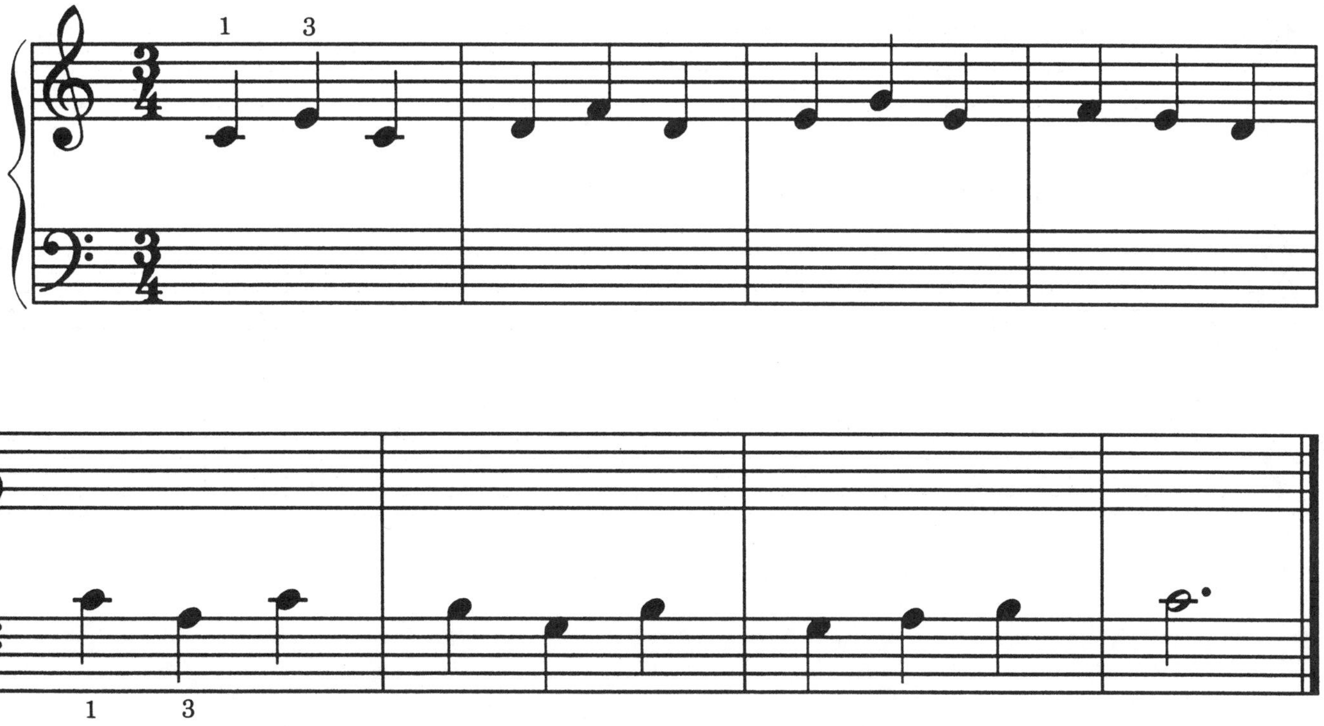

Variation for Number 26: Play both hands two octaves lower than written.

27. Broken Thirds Workout

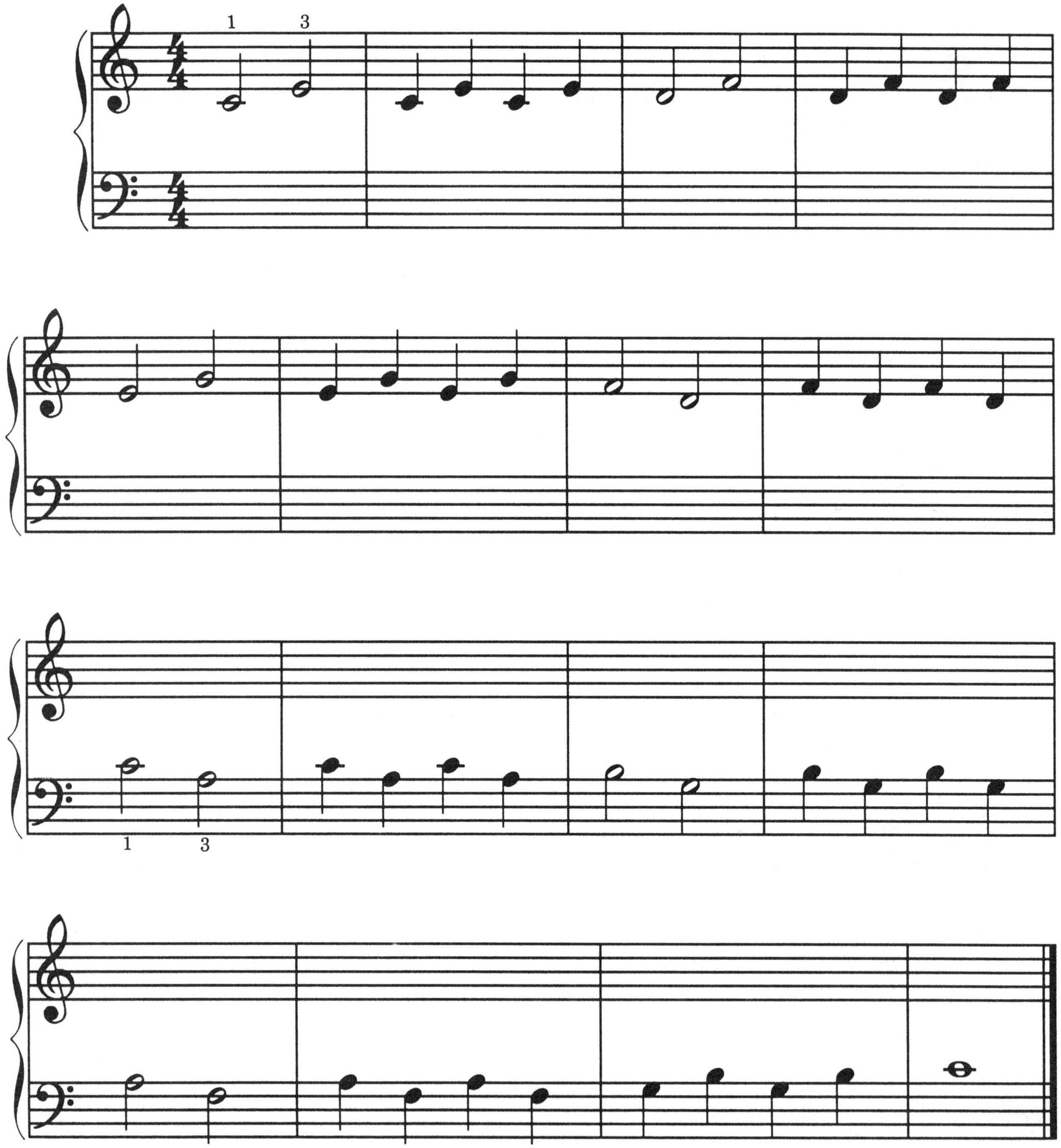

Create your own variation for Number 27.

28. Broken Triads in 4/4

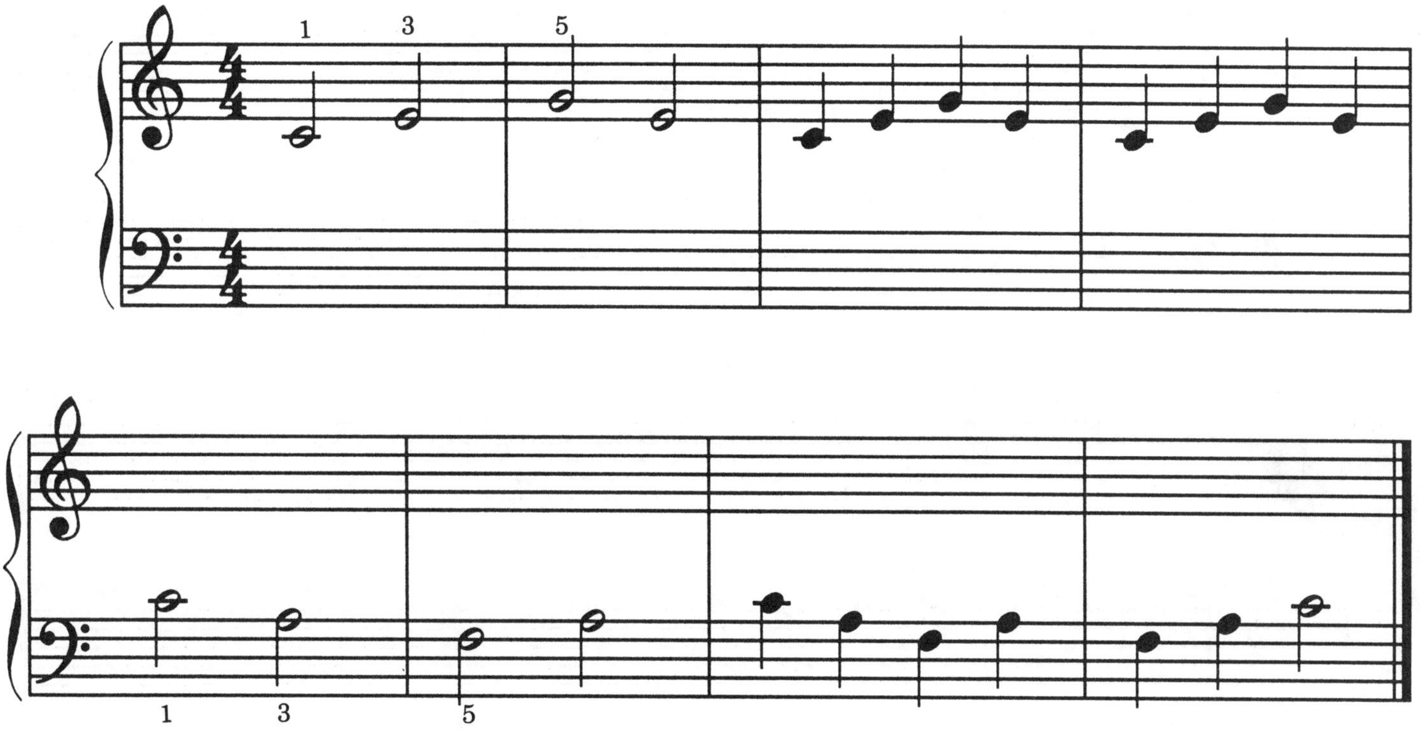

29. Broken Triads in 3/4

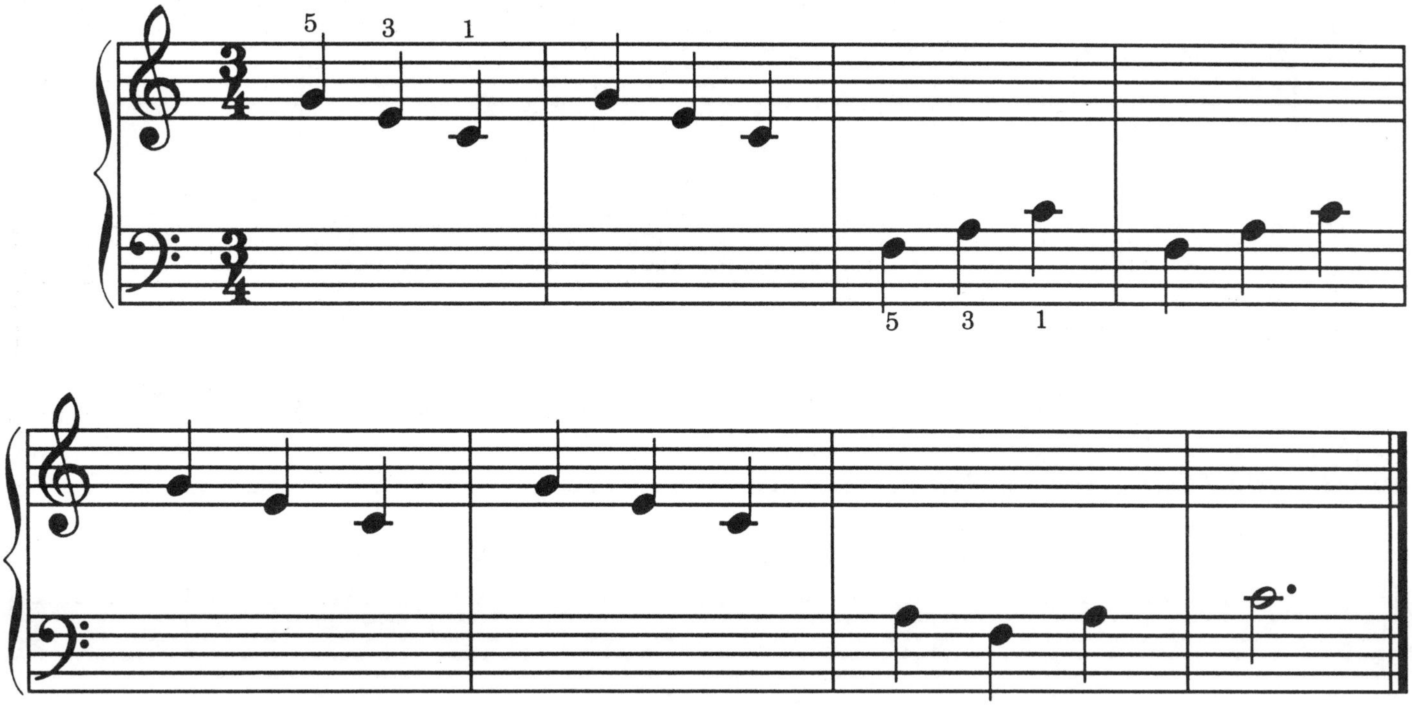

30. One Measure Pattern

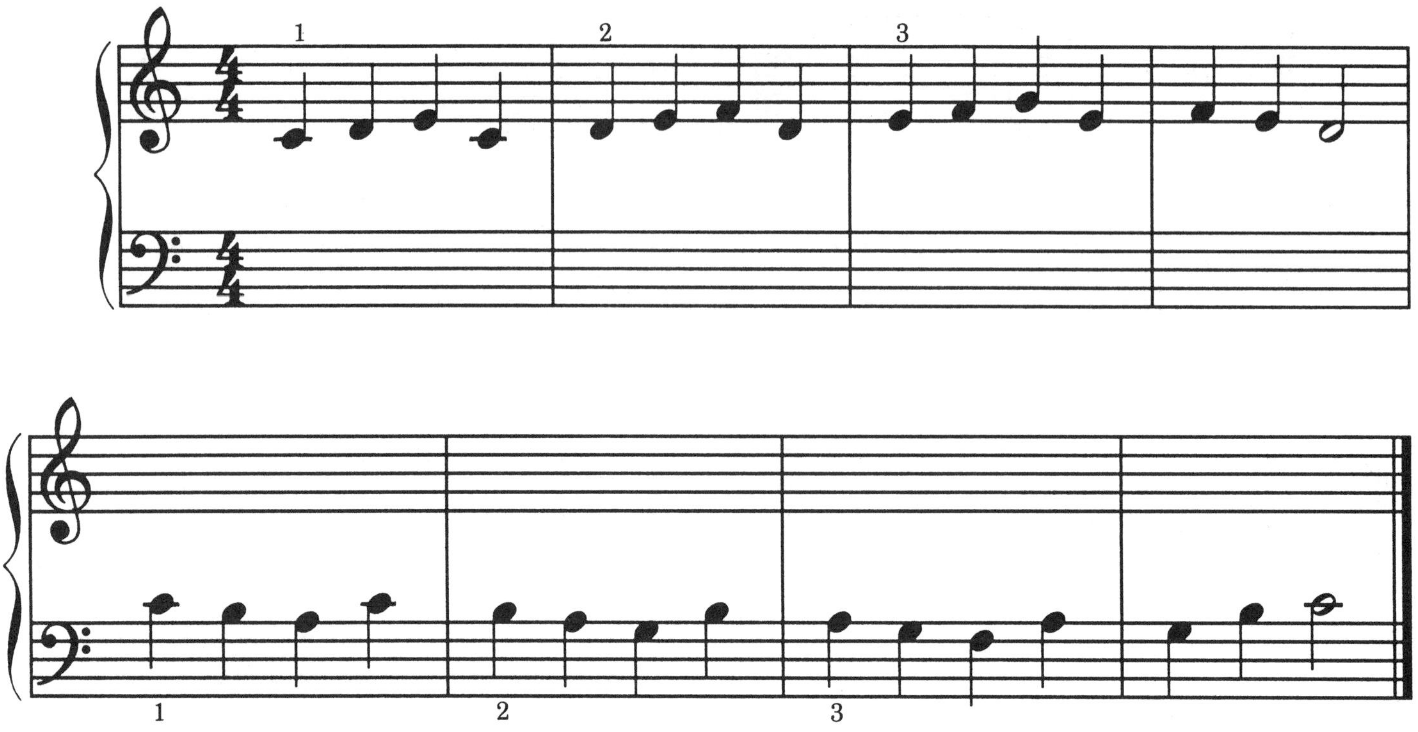

31. Changing Patterns

32. Two Measure Pattern

Variation for Number 32: Play the right hand one octave lower than written, and the left hand one octave higher than written. (Cross your left hand over.)

33. Broken and Block Thirds

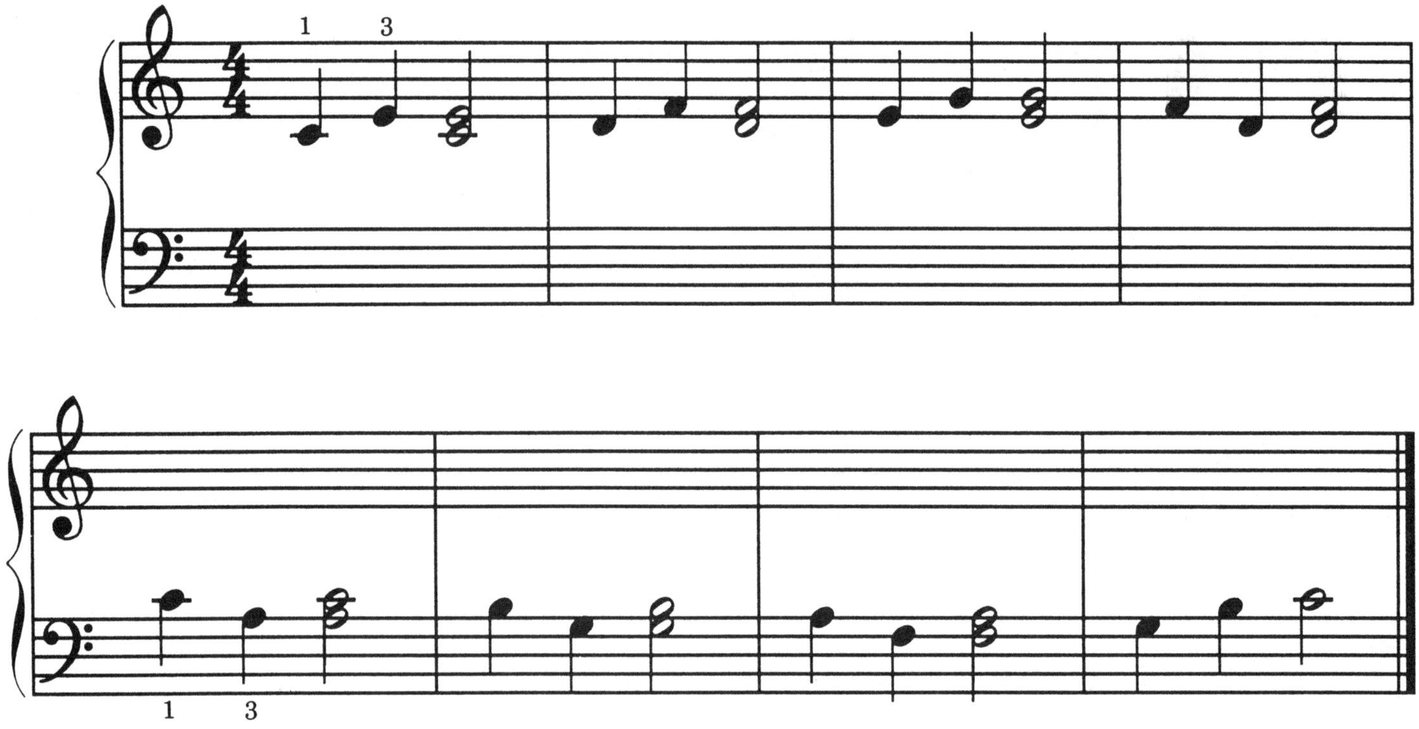

34. Step to Block Thirds

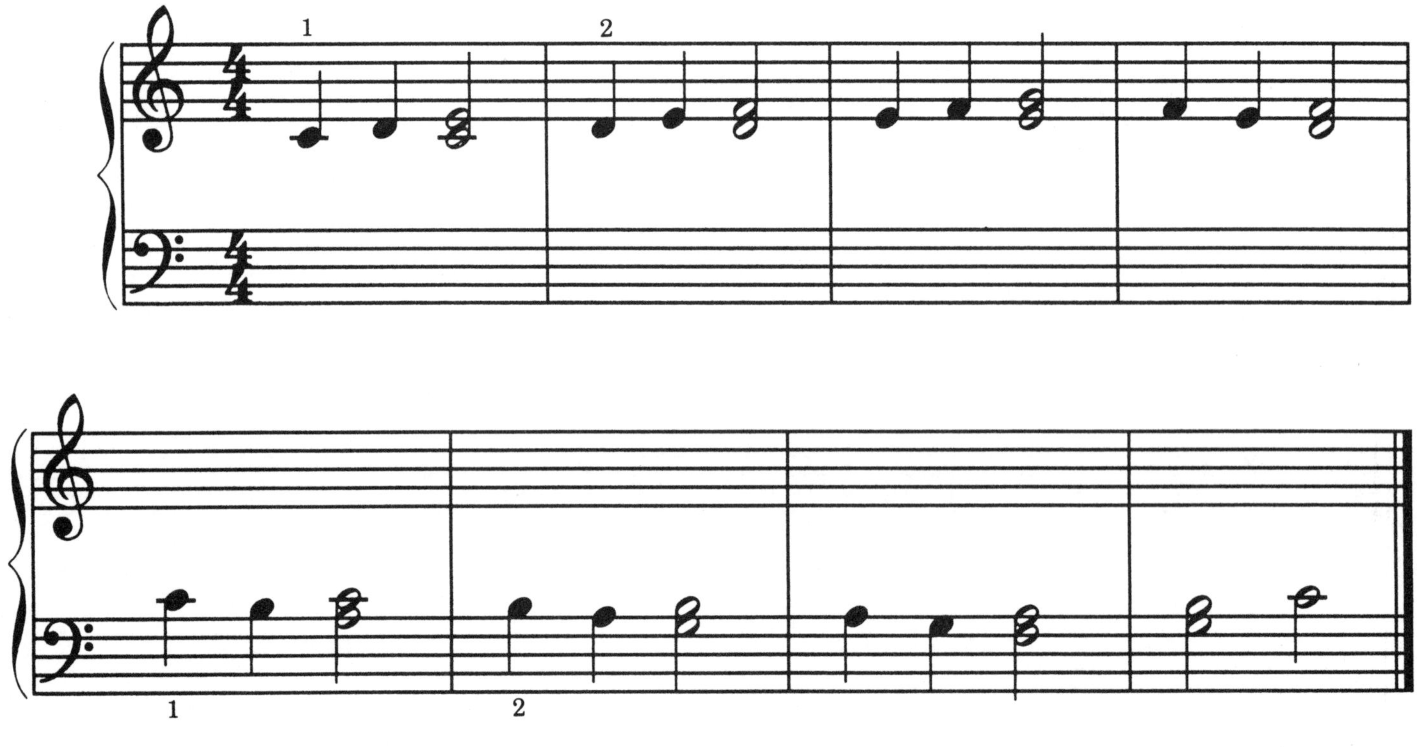

35. Legato and Staccato

36. Staccato Intervals

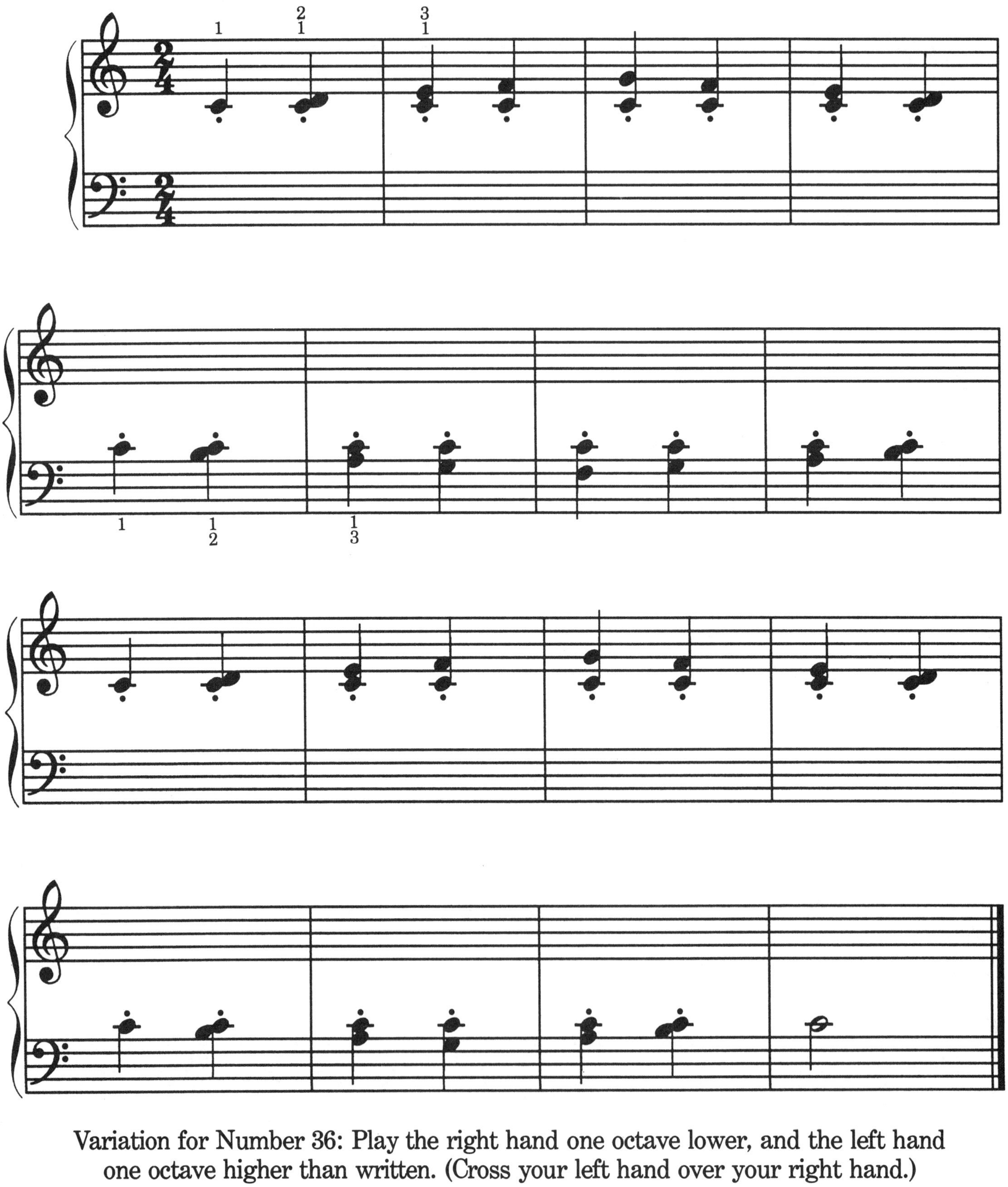

Variation for Number 36: Play the right hand one octave lower, and the left hand one octave higher than written. (Cross your left hand over your right hand.)

37. Staccato Interval Study

38. Legato and Staccato Phrases

39. Two-Note Slurs

40. Three-Note Slurs

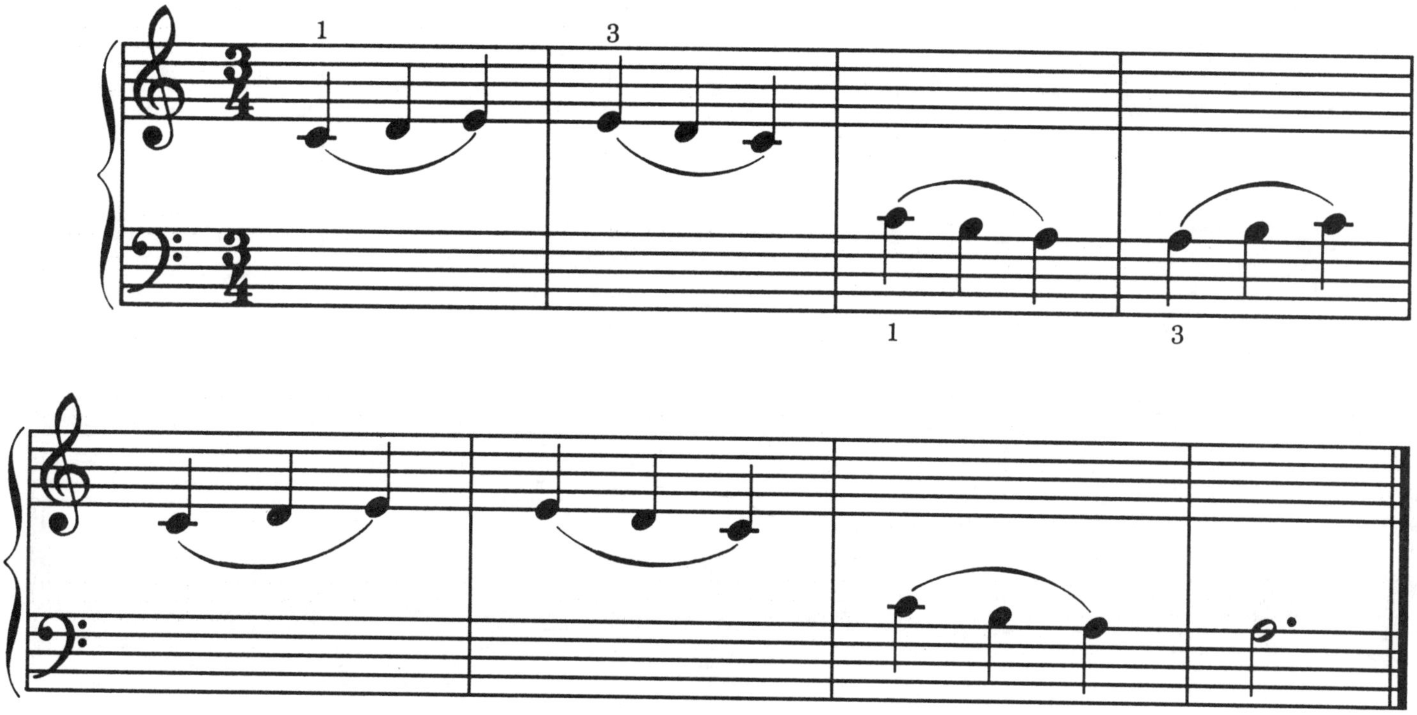

41. Four-Note Slurs

42. All Sharps

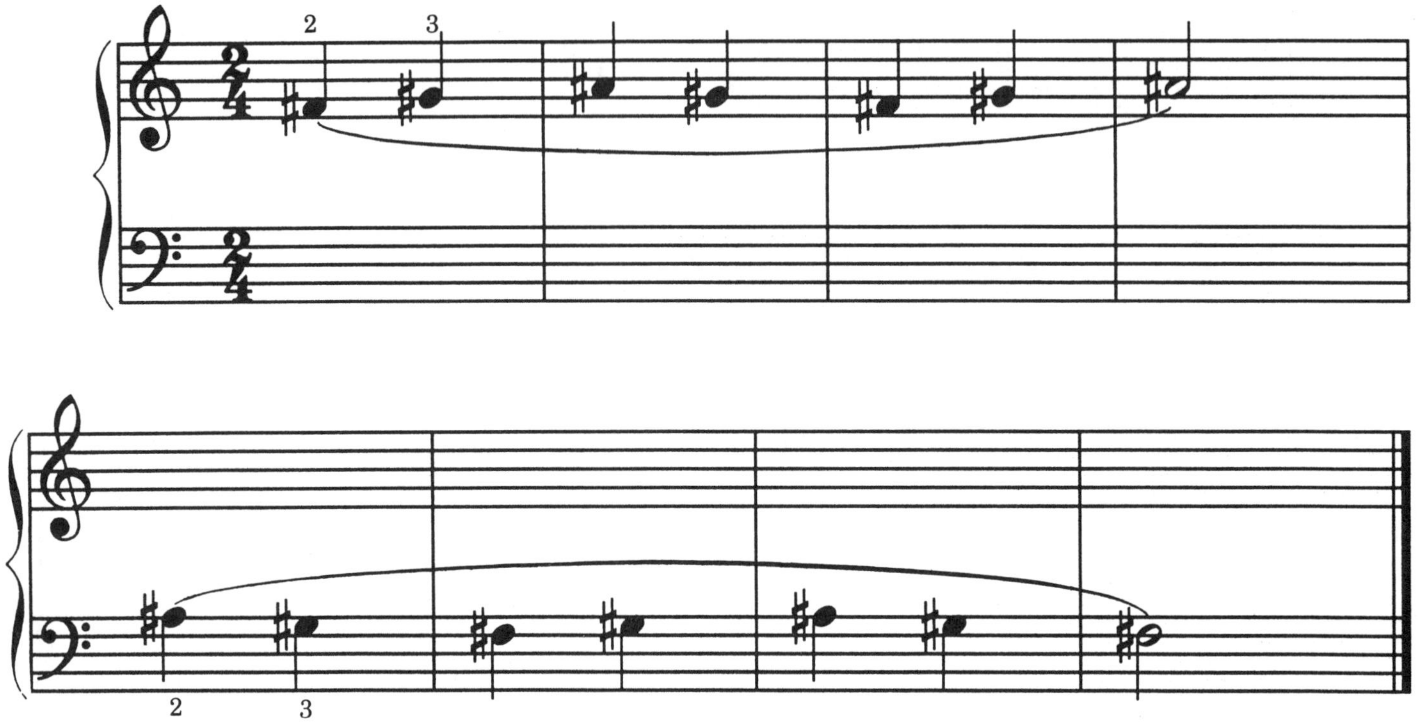

43. Minor and Major Descending Pattern

Variation for Number 43: Play both hands one octave lower than written.

44. All Flats

45. Major and Minor Ascending Pattern

Variation for Number 45: Play both hands one octave higher than written.

46. Legato Phrases Between the Hands